FOLLOWING CHRIST

Prayers from
IMITATION OF
CHRIST
in the Language
of Today

D1601275

FOLLOWING CHRIST

Prayers from IMITATION OF CHRIST in the Language of Today

Ronald Klug

Illustrated by Kathy Counts

Publishing House
St. Louis

Copyright © 1981 Concordia Publishing House
Manufactured in the United States of America

Library of Congress Cataloging in Publication Data

Klug, Ron.
    Following Christ.

    1. Prayers.   I. Imitatio Christi.   II. Title.
BV237.K58   242'.8   80-25260
ISBN 0-570-03826-X (pbk).

For Theodore Hartwig
who introduced me to the
Imitation of Christ

Introduction

For more than five centuries, Christians of all denominations have found guidance and strength and comfort in the devotional classic, the Imitation of Christ. Some have said it is the most widely read Christian book after the Bible. Among those who have acknowledged their debt to the Imitation are Thomas More, Ignatius Loyola, John Wesley, Dr. Samuel Johnson, and Dag Hammarskjold. Matthew Arnold called the book, "The most exquisite document, after those of the New Testament, of all that the Christian spirit has ever inspired."

The Imitation of Christ was written about 1427 by Thomas à Kempis, a member of the Brethren of the Common Life, a group of clergy and lay people whose purpose was to deepen the religious life of the time and to promote sound learning. The book was written to encourage people to follow the teachings of Christ and to imitate His life. At first, handwritten copies were made and circulated, until 1472, when it was set in type for the first time. It quickly spread across Europe; 1,800 editions and translations were in circulation by 1779.

The Imitation of Christ is divided into four books. Book I contains general counsel on the Christian life. Books II and III give further advice on the inner life of devotion. Book IV deals with the Sacrament of Holy Communion.

Scattered throughout the four books, but especially in Book III, are prayers of great dignity and simple strength—prayers of confession, praise, longing for God, and love of God. These prayers still speak for us today because they deal with the basic relationship of the soul with God. They can help us put into words our deepest longing for God and for His help.

I have gathered these prayers from the Imitation and paraphrased them into the language of today. In some cases I have divided very long prayers into several shorter ones. I have condensed some prayers by eliminating repetitions. I have tried always to remain faithful to the original spirit and meaning.

Several things strike me about these prayers.

1. They are profoundly Biblical. One often hears echoes of the words of Jesus, of the Psalms, and of the prophets. Someone has counted 850 Scripture passages that are quoted or alluded to in the Imitation.

2. The prayers are God-centered. Their dominant note is adoration. They magnify God, praising His greatness over against man's littleness, and His goodness over against man's sin. They emphasize the majesty of God far above all created things.

The Imitation has been criticized for taking too low a view of creation. This may be true, yet I wonder if today, when there is so much emphasis on self and on material things, this is not a voice calling us back to sanity. Perhaps this emphasis on the transcendence of God is a corrective to our frenzied search for self-fulfillment, luxuries, and pleasures. Over against all that, the Imitation cries, "God alone, above all things."

3. The prayers express man's total dependence on God. They echo the words of Jesus, "Without Me you can do nothing." They confess our estrangement from God, the coldness of our devotion, and the weakness of our will apart from God. They look to God and seek His help in every need.

8

4. The prayers focus on the soul's relationship to God. There is in them a concern for sound teaching and a gratitude for Word and Sacrament. There is a concern for Christian morality and for relationships with other people. But above all, the prayers speak of the individual in his personal relationship with God.

5. The prayers breathe a spirit of love. They delight in God's love for us and sing the believer's love for God. A friend of mine said, "When I read a book like this, I realize how little I love God."

My prayer for you is that these prayers, written so long ago, may live for you. May they speak to you and enable you to speak to God, the God who loves you, who has given you life, who has redeemed you from sin and death, and who empowers you daily with His Spirit. To Him be glory and honor to all ages.

O my Lord Jesus,
trusting completely in Your goodness
and great mercy,
I come to You
as a sick man comes to one who can heal,
as a hungry and thirsty man to the Fountain of Life,
as a needy man to the King of Heaven,
as a servant to his Lord,
as a creature to his Creator,
and as a desolate person to his kind and blessed Comforter.
You know well enough
that I have no goodness of my own to merit Your blessing.
Therefore I confess my unworthiness,
I acknowledge Your goodness,
I praise Your kindness,
and I give thanks for Your boundless love.

All that I am and all that I have
are Yours, O Lord.
Yet it is really You who serve me
rather than I You.
The heaven and earth,
the stars and planets,
and all that is in them
obey your laws day by day—
all in our service.
You have even appointed the angels
as our servants.
But above all this,
You Yourself stoop to serve us,
and You have promised to give Yourself to us.

How then can I repay You for all this goodness?
If only I could serve You faithfully all the days of my life!
If only I could serve You as I wish for even one day!
For You alone are worthy of all honor,
service, and praise
forever.
You are truly my Lord and my God,
and I Your poor servant
bound to serve You with all my powers
and to praise You without weariness.
This is my wish and desire,
that I may always glorify and praise You.
Therefore, O Lord, I ask You to supply
whatever is lacking in me,
for it is a great honor and glory to serve You
and to love You above all else.
For those who freely enter Your service
are richly blessed;
and those who discipline themselves for Your sake
receive the comfort of the Holy Spirit;
and those who enter on the narrow way,
find great freedom of spirit.

Help me, Lord Jesus, to rest in You
above all created things,
above all health and beauty,
above all glory and honor,
above all dignity and power,
above all knowledge and riches,
above all joy and gladness,
above all fame and praise,

Kathy Counts

above all sweetness and comfort,
above all hope and promise,
above all merit and desire,
above all gifts and favors You may send,
above all angels and archangels and all the hosts of heaven,
above all things visible and invisible,
and above everything
that is not Yourself,
O my God.

Lord, I know that nothing can comfort me,
nor can I rest content in anything created,
but in You alone, O my God,
whom I long to see eternally.
I cannot see You now
while I am in this earthly life,
but I must trust You patiently.
During the time they lived here
Your holy saints,
who now rejoice with You in heaven,
waited the coming of Your glory
with great faith and patience.
What they believed,
I too believe.
What they hoped to enjoy,
I too hope to enjoy.
Where by your grace they have arrived,
I too hope to come.
Until then I walk in faith,
strengthened by their example.

Until then I have the Holy Scriptures
for my comfort and the mirror of my life,
and I have for my refuge and remedy
Your most holy Sacrament.
I realize that there are two things
especially necessary for me in this world;
without them this life would be unbearable.
I need food and light.
These You have given me:
Your blessed Sacrament for the refreshment of my soul and body
and Your Word as a lamp to my feet
to show me the way I shall go.
Without these two gifts,
I cannot live well.
For the Word of God is the light of my soul,
and Your Sacrament is the bread of my life.

Lord, You know what is best for me.
Give me what You will
and when You will
and as much as You will.
Do with me as You know best
and as it pleases You
and brings You the most honor.
Place me where You will
and guide me according to Your wisdom.
I am in Your hand
as Your servant
ready to do all that You command.
I want to live,

not for myself,
but for You alone.
I want to live worthily
and profitably
and to Your honor.

༄

My Lord and my King,
how wonderful are the joys
You keep for those who fear You!
How much more will You give those
who love and serve You with all their hearts!
You give them the inexpressible joy of contemplation.
You showed Your love for me especially
by creating me when I was not,
and when I wandered far from You,
you led me back again to serve You
and taught me to love You.
O Fountain of eternal love,
how can I forget You,
since You have remembered me so lovingly?
When I was lost,
You showed Your mercy on me
beyond all I could have hoped or desired.
You sent me Your grace and love
above all my merits.
What shall I give You in return for all this goodness?
It is no great burden to serve You,
whom all creation is bound to serve.
Rather, it should seem a great wonder
that You would receive into Your service someone like me
and count me among Your beloved servants.

16

O Lord, by the inordinate love I had for myself,
I lost You
and myself as well.
Now in seeking You again,
I have found both myself
and You.
Therefore
I will humble myself all the more
and seek You more diligently.
Dear Lord, You give me more than I deserve,
more than I can ask or even hope for.
Your generosity and goodness never cease to bless
even those who are ungrateful
or who have wandered far from You.
Turn our hearts to You, O Lord,
that we may be thankful, humble, and devoted to You.
For You alone are our help,
our power,
and our strength.

Most kind Lord Jesus,
grant me Your grace.
Let it be always with me
and work in me
and preserve me to the end.
Grant that I may always desire and will
whatever is most pleasing and acceptable to You.
Let Your will be mine,

and let my will always follow Yours and conform to it.
Grant that I may die to all selfish ambition,
and for Your sake be willing to be despised and unknown.
Grant me above all else,
to find in You perfect peace and rest
for my body and soul.
For apart from You
everything is hard and restless.
In the true peace which is in You,
the one supreme and endless good,
I will live and find my rest.

O Lord of love,
You know my many weaknesses and needs,
the many sins that afflict me,
and how often I am discouraged, tempted,
troubled, and defiled.
I come to You for healing,
and I pray for Your strength.
Lord, You know all things,
to You my inward thoughts are open,
and You alone can perfectly guide and help me.
You know what I need,
and You understand all my shortcomings.
Lord, I come to You like a poor beggar,
asking for Your help.
Please give this beggar spiritual food.
Warm my coldness by the fire of your love.
Illumine my blindness by the light of Your presence.
Turn all worldly things to bitterness for me,
all irritating and frustrating things into patience,

and help me to turn away from everything harmful.
Lift up my heart to You in heaven,
and do not abandon me to wander on the earth.
You alone are my food and drink,
my love and my joy,
and my highest good.

❧

Lord, all You say is true.
May it be done to me according to Your Word.
Let Your truth teach me and guard me
and lead me to a blessed end.
May it free me from every wrong desire
and from all misdirected love.
Then I will walk with You
in freedom of spirit
and in liberty of heart.

❧

My God and my love,
You are mine, and I am Yours.
Deepen Your love in me, O Lord,
that I may learn how joyful it is to serve You.
Let Your love take hold of me
and raise me above myself,
that I may be filled with devotion
because of Your goodness.
Then I will sing to You the song of love.
I will follow You,
and my soul will never grow tired of praising You.

Let me love You more than myself,
and love myself only for Your sake.
Let me love all others
In You and for You,
as Your law of love commands.

Lord, help me in my troubles,
for human help is unpredictable.
Often I have found no friendship
where I expected it.
and often I have found friendship
where I least expected it.
I have decided it is useless
to trust in people,
for certain trust and help is found alone in You, O Lord.
In all that happens to us, we bless You, O Lord our God.
We are weak and unstable and easily deceived.
None of us can guard himself so carefully
that he does not fall into doubt or deception.
But whoever trusts in You, O Lord,
and seeks You with a pure heart,
does not easily fall away from You.
And if he encounters any trouble,
no matter how great,
he will soon be delivered by You and strengthened,
for You never forsake those who trust in You.
Rare is a faithful friend
who stands by through all troubles.
But You, Lord, are faithful in all things,
and there is none like You.

O Lord, what can I trust in this life?
And what is my greatest comfort on earth?
It is You, O Lord,
whose mercy is without limit.
Where have I ever done well without You?
And when have I ever been harmed when You were present?
I would rather be poor with You,
than rich without You.
I would rather be a wanderer on earth with You,
than to be in heaven without You.
For where You are,
there is heaven.
And where You are not,
there is death and hell.
You are all that I desire;
therefore I will earnestly pray to You.
There is no one who can help me
except You alone, O my God.
For You are my hope,
You are my trust,
You are my strength,
You are my comfort,
and my most faithful helper
in every need.

Speak, Lord, and I will gladly hear You.
Do not let Moses or the other prophets speak to me,
but rather You Yourself,

Kathy Counts

who gives inspiration and light to the prophets.
You alone, without them, can teach me perfectly;
but without You, they can do little for me.
The prophets can speak Your word,
but they cannot give me the Spirit.
They may speak eloquently,
but if You are silent,
they cannot set the heart on fire.
They teach the letter,
but You open the understanding.
They reveal spiritual mysteries,
but You unlock the meaning of the secrets.
They teach us Your commandments,
but You help us obey them.
They point the way,
but You give us the strength to walk in it.
They work outwardly,
but You illuminate and instruct the heart within.
Therefore speak to me Yourself, O living Truth,
so that I do not die without bearing fruit,
being warned from the outside,
but not warmed from within.
For I will be more strictly judged
if I have heard Your Word,
but have not obeyed it;
if I have known it,
but not loved it;
if I believe it,
but do not keep it.
Therefore, speak to me Yourself.
You have the words of eternal life.
Speak them to me and comfort my soul.
Transform my life to Your everlasting joy, honor, and glory.

O God, living Truth,
make me one with You
in perfect love.
Without You
all that I read or hear or see
is wearisome to me.
In You
is all I will or can desire.
Let all learned ones be silent before You;
let the whole creation be quiet,
so that You alone, O Lord,
may speak to my soul.
The more I am united with You,
the more I can understand,
for from You, O Lord,
I receive light and understanding.

What are we to You, O Lord?
Can the clay glorify itself
against the one who shapes it?
Can a person whose heart is subject to God's truth
be deceived by empty words?
The whole world could not lift up to false pride
one who is subject to God.
Nor could the one who has fixed his whole hope in God
be moved by flattering tongues.
He knows that those who speak empty words
are nothing; they will pass away

as quickly as the sound of their words.
But the truth of the Lord stands forever.

❧

O Lord, my God,
You are all my riches,
and everything I have is from You.
You alone are good, just, and holy.
You put all things in order,
You give all things,
and fill all things with Your goodness.
Remember Your mercies, Lord,
and fill my heart with Your grace.
How can I endure the miseries of this life
unless You comfort me with Your mercy and grace?
Do not turn Your face from me,
do not refuse to come to me.
If You withdraw Your Spirit from me,
my soul will become like a waterless desert,
useless to You.
You, Lord, are all my wisdom and learning.
Before the world was made
and before I was born,
You knew me,
and You know me now as I am.
Teach me, Lord, to do Your will
and to live worthily and humbly before You.

❧

Lord, I bring before You
the needs of my parents, friends,
brothers, sisters,
all who love me,
and all who have asked me to pray for them.
I pray that they may experience Your help
and the gift of Your comfort,
Your protection from all dangers,
and Your deliverance from all sin
that, freed from all evils,
they may give You high praise
in spiritual joy.
I also bring before You
all those who have in any way
hindered or burdened me
or who have done me any harm.
I also remember those
whom I have hurt or offended or troubled
in word or deed,
knowingly or unknowingly.
Lord, in Your mercy, forgive all our sins against one another.
Take from our hearts
all suspicion, hard feelings,
anger, dissension,
and whatever else may diminish the holy love
we should have for one another.
Have mercy, O Lord, on all who ask Your mercy.
Give grace to all who need it,
that we may finally come to everlasting life.

Lord, I know that You sometimes permit
trouble and temptation to come to me.
I cannot escape them,
but, driven by my need,
I must come to You for help
that You may work this out for my good.
O God, I feel uneasy and depressed
because of this present trouble.
I feel trapped on every side,
yet I know I have come to this hour,
so that I may learn that You alone
can free me from this predicament.
Lord, deliver me,
for what can I do without you,
helpless as I am?
Lord, give me patience in all my troubles.
Help me, and I will not be afraid,
no matter how discouraged I may be.
Help me to bear this trouble patiently
until the storm has passed
and my heart is calm again.
Your power, Lord, can take this trouble from me,
as You have done many times before.
No matter how hard it is for me,
It is easy for You, O Lord.

O Lord, when will all these miseries come to an end?
When will I be set free from the bondage of sin?
When will my mind be fixed on You alone?
When will the fullness of Your joys be mine?
When will I enjoy true freedom of mind and body?

When will I have true peace,
untroubled and secure,
inward and outward?
O Lord Jesus, when will I stand before You?
When shall I have a full vision of Your glory?
When will You be to me all in all?
When will I be with You in Your kingdom
which You have prepared from eternity
for those You have chosen?

I am left here, O Lord, a poor exile in the land of my enemies,
where there is constant war and great calamities.
Comfort me in my exile and ease my sorrow,
for my whole desire and longing is for You alone.
Everything the world offers me for comfort
is only another burden.
I long for spiritual growth
but I cannot achieve it.
I want to hold on to spiritual things,
but my daily worries and undisciplined desires
always pull me down.
I want my mind to rise above these concerns,
but my body holds me captive.
Thus I fight within myself;
for my spirit longs for heaven,
but my body holds on to earth.
Do not abandon me, O Lord.
Break the power of the Enemy over me.
Enable me to discipline my mind
and the powers of my soul.
Help me to forget all worldly things

and to reject all temptations to sin.
Help me, everlasting Truth,
so that no worthless things may have power over me.
Come, heavenly sweetness,
and let all bitterness of sin fall from me.

O Lord, Your providence
will order my life much better
than all I can do or say for myself.
Whenever I do not put all my trust in You,
I find only insecurity.
Lord, keep my will steadfast and true to You,
for I know that everything You plan for me is good.
If it is Your will that I be in the light,
blessed be Your name.
If it is Your will that I be in darkness,
may You also be blessed.
If You choose to comfort me,
blessed be Your name.
And if You wish me to live in trouble and without comfort,
may You be equally blessed.
Lord, I will gladly bear
whatever You allow to happen to me.
From Your hand I will gladly accept
good and bad,
sweet and bitter,
gladness and sorrow.
In all circumstances
I will thank You.
Only keep me from sin, Lord,
and I will fear neither death nor hell.

As long as You do not reject me
and blot my name from the book of life,
then no trouble that comes
can ever harm me.

⚘

Lord, I have called You,
and I have longed for You.
Because You first moved me to seek You,
I am ready to forsake all things for You.
Blessed be Your name, O Lord,
for You have shown such goodness to me,
according to the richness of Your mercy.
What more can I say or do, Lord?
I can only humble myself in Your presence
and remember my own wrongdoing.
There is none like You, O Lord,
in heaven or earth.
All Your works are good;
all Your judgments are wise and just;
by Your providence all things are ruled.
Eternal praise and glory to You,
O Wisdom of the Father.
May my body and soul,
my tongue and my heart,
and all creation
join to praise and bless You.

⚘

Kathy Counts

Forgive me, Lord,
when in my prayers
I think of anything but You.
I confess that I am often led astray by many distractions,
and my mind wanders.
I think about whatever comes into my head,
and what comes in are the things I love.
For whatever is immediately delightful
or has become pleasant by habit
is what comes readily to mind.
For this reason, You, who are the Truth, have said,
"Where your treasure is,
there will your heart be."
Therefore if I love heaven,
I think readily of heavenly things.
If I love the world,
I think about its pleasures and worry about its problems.
If I love my body,
I think about what is pleasing to the flesh.
If I love my spirit,
I think of that which contributes to my spiritual welfare.
For whatever it is I love,
that I am eager to think and speak about.
Blessed is the person
who for Your sake,
is free from all attachment to things
and has disciplined himself,
overcoming his natural inclinations
and crucifying the flesh by the power of the Spirit,
in order that he might offer his prayers
to You with a quiet mind.

O Lord, I have great need of Your grace
in fullest measure,
if I am to overcome my natural tendency to sin.
For while I inwardly agree with Your commandments
knowing they are good, just, and holy,
and that all sin is evil and to be avoided,
yet I often yield to sin
when I follow my senses rather than reason.
While I will to do good,
I do not have the strength to follow.
I make many good resolutions,
but because of my own weakness,
I fall back and fail
and can make no progress.
O Lord, how necessary, therefore, is Your help,
if I am to begin well, to continue well, and to end well.
For without You I can do nothing good,
but in You and by the power of Your grace,
all things are possible.

O Father, ever to be praised,
the time of trial has come for me,
and it is right that I should suffer something for You.
This is a time, known to You from eternity,
in which I will seem for a while to be utterly defeated.
Yet let me inwardly feel Your presence.
I will be despised by people, humiliated,
broken by sickness and suffering,
but I will rise again in the light of a new dawn
and receive glory in Your heavenly kingdom.
O Holy Father, You have planned it to be so,

and it is done as You have commanded.
To Your friends You give this privilege:
for love of You to suffer and be troubled in the world.
Nothing is done on earth
without Your guidance or permission.
Lord, it is good that I have been humbled,
that I may learn to know Your just judgments
and to banish all conceit and presumption from my heart.
It is for my profit that I have been humiliated,
that I may learn from it
to seek help and comfort from You
rather than from men.

O Lord, You are always the same,
and always will be the same—
always good, just, and holy,
always ordering all things
according to Your loving wisdom.
But I, always more prone to evil than to good,
never remain the same,
but change many times a day.
Yet when You touch me with Your helping hand,
things are better for me.
For You alone,
with no human aid,
can help and strengthen me,
so that I will no longer be unstable,
but be wholly fixed in You
and there find perfect rest.

Open my heart to know Your law
and teach me to walk in Your commandments.
Give me grace to understand Your will
and to remember Your many blessings,
so that I may give You proper thanks for them.
I know and confess
that I am not yet able
to give You fitting thanks,
for the least benefit You have given me,
for I am smaller than Your smallest gift.
When I consider Your boundless generosity,
my spirit reels before its greatness.

I thank You, Lord,
that You have not ignored my sin,
but have punished me with the scourges of love
and have sent me sorrows and troubles
within and without.
Heavenly Physician of the soul,
You wound and heal,
You cast down,
and raise up again,
so that I may learn the littleness of my own power
and may trust more fully in You.
O Lord, Your discipline teaches me,
Your wounding heals me.
Make me a humble disciple,
that I may walk according to Your will.
To You I commit myself and all I am.
You know all things,
and nothing is hidden from You.
You know what is helpful for me,

and how trouble helps to scour away the rust of sin.
Do not reject me because of my sinful life,
which is well known to You,
but do with me according to Your good pleasure.

༄

O Lord God, most just judge,
strong and patient,
who understands our weakness and wickedness,
be my strength and comfort in every need.
My own conscience is inadequate,
but You understand what is unknown to me.
Therefore I should humble myself
under all criticism
and patiently endure all things in love.
Forgive me, Lord,
for the many times I have failed in this,
and give me greater patience
in the future.
I can obtain pardon only by believing in Your mercy,
not by trusting in my own works
or by defending my own innocence.
Although I may not be conscious of any fault,
I still cannot justify myself.
If You withhold Your mercy,
no one can be justified in Your sight.

༄

Men seek their own interest,
but You, Lord, seek only my salvation and welfare,

and You turn all things to my good.
Even if You permit me to be tempted and troubled,
You still do this for my good.
In times of trial like this,
You are as worthy of my praise
as when You fill me with spiritual comfort.
In You, then, Lord, I place my whole trust.
In You I bear patiently all my troubles,
for without You I find only instability and weakness.
Many worldly friends will be no help;
powerful advocates are useless;
wise counselors have no helpful advice;
learned books give no comfort,
and no secret place can defend me,
if You, Lord, are not by my side
to help, comfort, counsel, instruct, and defend.
All things that seem to bring happiness,
are worthless without You,
for they cannot give true and lasting happiness.
You alone are the source of all good things,
the fullness of life,
the depth of wisdom,
and our greatest comfort in every need.

O Lord, set me on fire with Your presence,
and turn me to Yourself
that I may be wholly dedicated to You.
Let me be united in spirit with You,
by the grace of inward union
and by the melting of burning love.
Do not send me away

hungry or thirsty,
but deal with me in Your mercy,
as You have dealt with Your servants in times past.
How marvelous it would be
if I were wholly on fire for You
and dead to self.
For You, Lord, are the fire unquenchable,
burning forever.
You are the love that purifies the heart
and enlightens the mind.

❧

O Lord, a truly devout person
begrudges all the attention spent on
food and drink and clothing and other bodily needs.
Help me to use these things with moderation,
and not be overly concerned about them.
It is not right or possible to ignore them,
for we must take care of our bodies.
But Your holy law forbids us
from craving luxuries
sought more for pleasure than for necessity.
I ask You, then, O Lord,
to govern and guide me
that I may learn to live simply at all times.

❧

O Lord, my God,
You are above all things.
You alone are most good,

most mighty, most sufficient,
most full of goodness,
most sweet and comforting.
You alone are most fair,
most able, and most glorious above all things.
In You all goodness is gathered together,
fully and perfectly,
now and forever.
Therefore, whatever You give me,
besides Yourself, O Lord,
is small and unsatisfying to me.
For my heart cannot rest or find perfect peace,
until it rises above all Your gifts
to rest in You alone.

Lord, make possible for me by grace
what is impossible to me by nature.
You know how little I can bear to suffer,
how quickly I am discouraged
by a little trouble.
I pray that I may accept and even love
all the troubles that You permit to come to me.
To suffer for You and be troubled for You
is good and profitable for my soul.

Lord, I confess my sinfulness
and acknowledge my weakness.
Often it is only a little thing

Kathy Counts

that defeats me
and makes me slow to do what is right.
Sometimes I resolve to stand firm,
but a little temptation comes,
and I quickly fall.
And when I feel most secure,
I am almost overcome by the smallest temptation.
Consider my weakness, O Lord,
for You know it better than anyone else.
Even when I do not yield to these temptations,
they trouble and disturb me,
and I grow weary of living constantly in conflict.
So I come to You for help, O Lord.
Strengthen me with spiritual strength,
so that the old enemy, the devil,
whom I must fight endlessly,
may have no power over me.
Strengthen me so that my flesh,
still not subject to the Spirit,
may not gain the upper hand.

Blessed may You be, heavenly Father,
Father of my Lord Jesus Christ,
for You remember me, Your poor servant,
and You comfort me with Your presence,
even though I am not worthy of it.
When You come into my heart, everything in me rejoices.
You are my glory,
the joy of my heart,
my hope and my refuge in time of trouble.
Because my love for You is still weak

and my virtue imperfect,
I have great need of Your strength and comfort.
Come to me often, therefore,
and teach me Your Word.
Set me free from false desires
and wrong attachments,
that I may be free and able to love You,
strong to suffer for You,
and firm to persevere in You.

Most loving God,
keep me from being overwhelmed
by the cares and busyness of this life.
Keep me, too, from being overly concerned
with the needs of my body
and from being enslaved by the pursuit of pleasure.
Save me, too, from the dangers to my spirit,
so that I am not crushed or overwhelmed
by depression or anxiety.
I do not ask to be delivered only from the emptiness
that so many pursue so desperately,
but also from the miseries that grieve my spirit,
burdened by all the suffering of humanity.
These miseries prevent me from experiencing Your presence
freely, whenever I would.
O Lord God, my joy above all joys,
turn to bitterness
all pleasures that draw me away from eternal joys.
Do not let flesh and blood overcome me,
nor the world with its brief glory deceive me,
nor the devil with all his cunning ensnare me.

Give me strength to resist,
patience to endure,
and constancy to persevere.
In place of all the pleasures of the world,
give me the rich comfort of Your Holy Spirit,
and in place of all worldly love,
send into my soul the love of Your holy name.

My Lord Jesus, do not be far from me,
but come quickly and help me
for evil thoughts have risen in my mind,
and I am terrified by fears for the future.
How shall I break their power over me?
How shall I go unhurt without your help?
O Lord,
You have promised,
"I myself will prepare your way,
leveling mountains and hills.
I will open the gates of the prison,
and reveal to you
the hidden treasures of spiritual knowledge."
O Lord, do as You have said,
and let Your coming
drive away all evil thoughts.
This is my hope and my only comfort—
to turn to You in every trouble,
to put all my trust in You,
to call inwardly upon You,
and to wait for Your comfort with patience.

O Lord, all that we have,
in body or soul,
without or within,
naturally or supernaturally,
are Your gifts
and reveal You
as a loving and good God.
And whether we receive more or less,
all are Your gifts,
and without You we would have nothing.

Whoever has received more
may not boast
as though he had received them because of his own merits,
or despise those who have received less.
He is greatest and most pleasing to You
who claims the least for himself
and who humbly and devoutly
returns You thanks for those gifts.
He who holds himself in humble esteem
and counts himself unworthy
is ready to receive from You the greater gifts.

Whoever has received fewer gifts
should not be sad or envious.
Rather he should lift his mind to You
and praise Your goodness,
because Your gifts are given
freely, generously, and lovingly,
without respect of persons.
You alone know what is right
for each person to receive.
All good things come from You,
and in all things You are to be praised.

My God and my All!
When You are with me,
all things are pleasant and joyful.
When You are absent,
all things are irritating and unsatisfying.
When You come,
You bring rest to my heart,
true peace, and new joy,
for nothing can give us lasting joy without You.
Whoever knows Your joy
will find joy in all things.
But whoever finds no joy in You,
will find no joy in anything.
The worldly wise and sensual-minded
fail to find wisdom,
for worldly wisdom is empty,
and sinful pleasures lead only to death.
Those who follow You
by leading a moderate and self-disciplined life
are truly wise.
They are led from illusion to truth
and from flesh to spirit.
They find delight in God,
and whatever good they find in created things,
they attribute to the glory and praise of God the Creator.
For they understand how great is the difference
between the creature and the Creator,
between time and eternity,
between light created and Light uncreated.

O Lord, I long for the joy of inward peace,
the peace of Your chosen children,
who are strengthened and refreshed by You.
Without Your help
I cannot find this peace.
When You withdraw Yourself from me,
as You sometimes have done,
I cannot follow the way of Your commandments.
Instead I feel crushed
because I no longer experience Your strength
which protects me from all temptations and dangers.
But if You come to me again
and fill my heart with peace and joy,
then my spirit will be full of song
and entirely devoted to Your praise.

O Lord God, heavenly Father,
blessed be Your name now and forever.
As You will,
so it is done,
and what You do
is always good.
Let me, your most unworthy servant,
rejoice in You
and not in myself
or in any other thing.
You alone, O Lord, are my joy,
my hope, and my crown,
my gladness, and my honor.
I have nothing that is not Your gift,
and I have no merit of my own.

Kathy Counts

All things that You have created
and that You have given
are Yours, O Lord.

᭥

O blessed Lord,
You make the poor in spirit rich in virtue,
and You make the rich humble in heart.
Come, descend on me.
Fill me with Your comfort
so that my soul may not faint
because of its weariness and dryness.
I pray, Lord, that I may find grace in Your sight,
for Your grace is sufficient for me,
even though I lack the things my nature desires.
Though I am troubled and tempted on every side,
I will fear no evil
as long as Your grace is with me.
Your grace is my strength, my comfort,
my counsel, and my help.
It is stronger than my enemies
and wiser than all the wise.
Your grace is the teacher of truth,
and the light of the heart,
and comfort in trouble.
It banishes sorrow,
drives away fear,
nourishes devotion,
and produces repentance.
Without grace, I am only a dry stick to be thrown away.
Therefore, O Lord, let Your grace always go before me
and follow me, through Your son Jesus Christ. Amen.

Strengthen me, O Lord God,
by the power of Your Holy Spirit.
Remove from me all groundless fears,
and give me inner courage.
Let me never be enticed away from You
by the desire for anything else,
but help me to realize
that all things are transitory—
as I am.
In this world nothing is lasting,
and everything is uncertain
and troubling to the spirit.
How wise is the one who understands this!
Give me true spiritual wisdom, Lord,
that I may learn to seek You,
and find You,
and above all to love You.
Enable me to understand all things as they really are.
May I wisely avoid all those who would flatter me
and deal patiently with those who irritate me.
True wisdom cannot be swayed by every wind of words,
and it disregards the cunning flattery of deceitful men.
If I live by this wisdom,
I will move forward on the road I must travel.

O Jesus, brightness of eternal glory,
joy and comfort of all Christian people,
who walk like pilgrims

in the wickedness of this world,
hear the silent cry of my heart:
"How long will my Lord delay His coming?"
Come to me, poor and little as I am,
and bring me joy.
Stretch out Your hand
and deliver me from all anguish and pain.
Come, Lord, come,
for without You
my soul is barren and empty.
Come, Lord, come,
for without You,
no day or hour is happy.
Without You,
my table is without its guest,
for You alone are my joy.
I am like a prisoner in chains
until through the light of Your presence,
You visit me to refresh me,
to liberate my spirit,
and to show me Your face as my friend.
Let others seek whom they will;
there is nothing I will seek,
nothing that can give me joy,
but You alone, My God,
my hope and my everlasting salvation.
I will not keep silent
or cease my prayer,
until You return to me,
and say to my soul,
"I am here."

Lord Jesus, send the clarity of Your light
into my mind
and expel all darkness from my heart.
Fight strongly for me
and drive away the temptations
that rage like wild beasts within me.
Then my conscience will be at peace,
and the praise of Your name
will sound within the temple of my soul.
Command the winds and storms of pride to be still,
and the sea of covetousness to be at rest.
Subdue the north wind of the devil's temptation.
Then there will be a great calm within me.

Lord Jesus, You were patient
in Your life on earth,
fulfilling the will of Your Father.
In the same way,
I wish to bear myself patiently,
accepting Your will
in all things.
I will bear the burdens of this life
as long as it is Your will.
Even though this life is hard,
Your grace makes it worthwhile.
By Your example and the examples of the saints,
this life is made easier for the weak,
and we are saved by Your blessed passion
and the atonement of Your sacred death.

Oh, what thanks we owe You
because You have showed us the true and holy way
to Your eternal kingdom.
Your life is our Way,
and by patience we will journey on to You,
our Leader and our Goal.
If You, Lord, had not gone before
and showed us the way,
who could follow?
How many would have lagged far behind,
if they had not had Your example as a guide?
Even now, after we have heard Your teachings
and seen Your mighty acts,
we are cold and dull.
What would we have done without them?
Surely we would have fixed our hearts and minds
only on the things of this world.
But now, O Lord, from this
may Your great goodness
preserve us.

Lord Jesus,
be with me
in every place and every time.
May I be willing to give up all earthly comfort
for the sake of Your comfort.
And when even Your comfort is lacking,
may I find consolation
by submitting to Your will
and accepting Your testing.
For You will not always be angry,
nor will You condemn me forever.

False pride is a dangerous sickness, O Lord,
for it draws us away from the true glory
we should have in You,
and robs us of heavenly grace.
When a man is self-satisfied,
he displeases You.
And when he seeks popularity,
he loses his integrity.
For true lasting joy is found not in self-glorification,
but in giving glory to You,
not in one's own strength,
but in Your name.
Therefore, may Your name, and not mine, be praised,
Your works, and not mine glorified.
You alone are my glory.
You alone are the joy of my heart.
I will offer You praise and glory every hour of the day,
but for myself, I will glory only in my weaknesses.
I will seek the glory that only God can give.
For all human glory,
all this world's honor,
all pride of position,
compared to Your glory,
are foolish and empty.
O blessed Trinity,
my God, my Truth, my Mercy,
to You be all praise, honor,
power, and glory,
through endless ages.

O Lord, there can be no goodness in us
if You withdraw Yourself.
No wisdom can benefit us,
if You cease to guide us.
No strength can preserve us,
if You no longer defend.
No purity can be secure,
if You do not guard it.
No watchfulness of our own can protect us,
if You do not keep watch.
If You abandon us,
we are soon lost and perish.
But if You come to us with Your grace,
we are lifted up to live again.
We are weak,
but You make us strong.
We are cold and dull,
but by You our hearts are warmed.

Help me, Lord, to know all I should know
and to love all I should love,
to value what most pleases You
and to reject what is evil in Your sight.
Let me not judge superficially according to what I see
nor be influenced by the opinions of the foolish,
but give me true judgment to discern
between things seen and unseen
and to seek Your good will and pleasure at all times.
Human judgment is often faulty,
and people are often deceived by loving only material things.
Is a person any better

just because others think highly of him?
For one deceitful person
deceives another.
The higher the flattery,
the greater the humiliation that follows.
No matter what his reputation before other people,
a man is worth only what he is in the sight of God,
that much and no more.

ಲ

O Lord Jesus Christ,
lover of the soul,
and Lord of creation,
who will give me wings of perfect liberty
that I may fly to You,
and be at rest?
When shall I be set free
and taste your sweetness, O Lord?
When shall I become so centered in You
that for love of you I may no longer
be conscious of myself,
but of You alone?
I trust that You will come to me,
as You come to all those who love You faithfully.
Now I often mourn and complain
about the miseries of this life,
for many evil things happen daily
that disturb me and darken my path.
They hinder me and distract me
so I cannot approach You freely
and enjoy Your gracious presence.
Wherefore I pray

that both my sadness and my desire
may move You to hear me, O Lord.

O everlasting Light,
far surpassing all created things,
pour forth the beams of Your brightness from above,
to purify, gladden, and enlighten me.
Quicken my spirit with all its powers
that it may hold to You with joy inexpressible.
Oh, when will that blessed hour come,
when You will fill me with your presence
and be to me all in all?
Until that gift is given
I can never know fulness of joy.
For my old nature is still strong within me;
it is not yet wholly crucified or entirely dead.
The flesh still fights against the spirit,
stirs up conflicts within me,
and does not allow me to live in peace.
But You, O Christ, are Lord over the power of the sea,
You can calm its raging waves.
Come and help me!
Break the power of the Enemy,
who stirs up this battle within me.
Show the strength of Your goodness,
for I have no hope or refuge but in You,
my Lord and my God.

Kathy Counts

My soul is like the primeval earth—
formless and empty and dark.
Send out the light of Your truth, O Lord.
Pour out Your grace
on my heart, dry and barren,
and bathe it in the dew of inward devotion.
Then my soul will bring forth good fruit,
agreeable and pleasing to You.
Inspire my mind
that is now weighed down by sin.
Raise my desire to the love of spiritual things,
so that having tasted heavenly joy,
I may turn from all the passing pleasures of the world.
Free me from all dependence on the temporary satisfaction
that comes from things which soon pass away,
for these can never fully satisfy my longings.
Unite me to You
by the unbreakable bonds of love,
for You alone can satisfy the one who loves You,
and without You,
the world is empty and worthless.

O Lord, how good and peaceful it is
to remain silent about others,
neither believing everything that is said,
nor repeating everything we see and hear.
We should not be blown about by every puff of words.
We should not open our hearts to all people,
but always seek You,
who understand us perfectly.
You desire that our whole lives,

inwardly and outwardly,
be ordered according to Your will.
A sure way of retaining spiritual grace
is to avoid people and things that lead us astray,
and to seek wholeheartedly
the things that bring fervor of spirit
and amendment of life.

O Lord, if I come to you
thinking myself better than I am,
my own sins witness against me.
But if I come humbly and honestly,
then Your grace will come to me
and Your light will brighten my heart
and give me true understanding of myself,
so that my pride will be drowned in the valley of meekness.
You show me my true self,
what I have been
and what I have become.
For I am nothing,
and did not know it.
Left to myself,
I will continue to be nothing
but if You help me only a little,
I will be strong again and filled with new joy.
I am amazed at how quickly You can pick me up
after I have fallen.
It is Your love, Lord,
that does this,
Your love that guides me,
helps me in all my needs,

guards me from many dangers,
and keeps me from unnumbered evils.

❧

Lord, I am not worthy of Your comfort
or Your spiritual visitation.
You would be just
if You left me needy and desolate.
But You, Lord, are kind and merciful,
and do not wish me to perish,
and so You comfort me
though I do not deserve it.
Although it is painful for me,
I will honestly confess my weaknesses and admit my defects
so that I may obtain Your mercy and forgiveness.
In my guilt and confusion,
what can I say?
Only this: "I have sinned, Lord, I have sinned.
Be merciful and forgive."
In true penitence and humility
the hope of pardon is found,
the troubled conscience is cleared,
and lost grace is restored.
We are spared God's anger,
and God and the penitent sinner
meet in the holy embrace of heavenly love.

❧

Lord, I have great need of Your grace,
if I am to reach the state

where no created thing
can keep me from perfect contemplation of You.
For as long as any transitory thing
enslaves me or holds me back,
I cannot come freely to You.
One who desired to come to You freely said,
"Who will give me wings like the dove,
that I may fly into the bosom of my Savior
and be at rest?"
Who is more at rest
than the man with a single purpose?
And who is more free
than the one who desires nothing on earth?

I come to You, O Lord,
that I may be blessed by Your gift,
rejoicing in the Feast
You have prepared for me.
In You I find all that I may or should desire,
for You are my Savior and my Redeemer.
You are my hope, my strength,
my honor and glory.
Let me find joy in You today, Lord,
for I have lifted my soul to You.
I wish to receive You with reverence and devotion:
I would invite You into my house,
as Zacchaeus did,
so that I too may receive Your blessing,
and be counted among Your chosen ones.
My soul desires to receive Your body and blood.
My heart longs to be united with You.

Give me Yourself,
and it is enough;
nothing but You can satisfy me.
Without You I cannot live.
Therefore I must often come to You
and receive You for my spiritual health.
For deprived of this heavenly food,
I would fall by the wayside.
I so often fall into sin.
Because I so quickly grow lukewarm and sluggish,
it is essential for me
to be cleansed and renewed by prayer and confession
and by receiving of Your holy Sacrament.
O Lord God, Creator and Giver of Life,
how wonderful is Your kindness and mercy to me
that You should stoop to visit so poor a creature as I
to refresh me, to satisfy my hunger
with Your whole divinity and humanity.
Happy is the man who devoutly receives You
with all spiritual joy.
How great a Lord he receives!
How beloved a Guest he welcomes into his house!
How delightful a Companion he receives!
How faithful a Friend he accepts,
who receives You!
For You alone are to be loved and desired
before and above all others.

To You, Father of mercy, I lift up my eyes.
In You alone, my God, I put my trust.
Bless and hallow my soul

that it may be Your heavenly dwelling.
Let nothing remain in my heart that will offend You.
Have mercy on me and hear the prayer of Your servant,
an exile in the country of the shadow of death.
Guard and keep me among the many dangers
of this corruptible life.
Through Your grace guide me
in the ways of peace
until I reach my home
of everlasting light.

Lord, blessed is Your Holy Word.
It is sweeter to my mouth than the honeycomb.
What would I do
in all my troubles and trials,
if You did not comfort and strengthen me
with Your holy and health-giving Word?
Therefore it does not matter
how many storms or troubled waters
I go through for Your sake,
so long as I come at last
to the port of everlasting salvation.
Give me a good end
and a joyful passage from this life.
Remember me,
my Lord and my God,
and lead me by a straight and ready way
into Your kingdom.